W9-ANU-102

DISCOVER
JELLYFISH

by Susan H. Gray

Cherry Lake Publishing • Ann Arbor, Michigan

Published in the United States of America
by Cherry Lake Publishing
Ann Arbor, Michigan
www.cherrylakepublishing.com

Content Adviser: Dominique A. Didier, PhD, Associate Professor,
Department of Biology, Millersville University
Reading Adviser: Marla Conn, ReadAbility, Inc

Library of Congress Cataloging-in-Publication Data
Gray, Susan Heinrichs.
  Discover jellyfish / Susan H. Gray.
    pages cm
  Includes bibliographical references and index.
  Audience: Ages 6 to 10.
  Audience: Grades K to 3.
  ISBN 978-1-63362-600-3 (hardcover)—ISBN 978-1-63362-780-2 (pdf)—
ISBN 978-1-63362-690-4 (pbk.)—ISBN 978-1-63362-870-0 (ebook)
  1. Jellyfishes—Juvenile literature. I. Title.

  QL377.S4G7265 2015
  593.5'3—dc23

                                        2015005395

Cherry Lake Publishing would like to acknowledge the work of the Partnership
for 21st Century Skills. Please visit www.p21.org for more information.

Printed in the United States of America
Corporate Graphics

TABLE OF CONTENTS

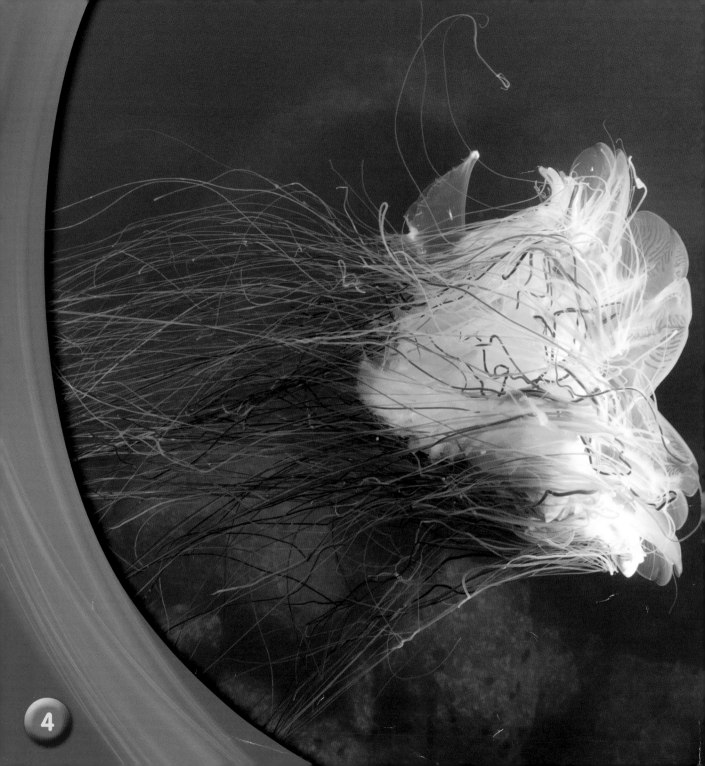

What Is It?

Look at this picture. Is this thing a plant or an animal? It is an animal that lives in the sea. It is not a fish. And it is not made of jelly. But it is called a jellyfish!

Jellyfish don't have fins, unlike most other swimming animals.

6

Jellyfish live in the ocean. They like water that is salty. Some live in very cold water. Big chunks of ice float there. Other jellies live in warm water. They **drift** around in the sunlight. Boats often bump into them.

Some jellyfish live in shallow water.

Sometimes people see big groups of jellies. These are called **swarms**. A swarm may have thousands of jellyfish. The jellies bump and bash into each other. But it does not hurt them.

CREATE!

You know that jellyfish are not really fish. But imagine that you had to give these animals a name. Make a list of names you would give them.

The jellyfish in this swarm glow in the dark.

Life of the Jellyfish

A jellyfish has a soft, mushy body. The main part is called the **bell**. It is shaped like an umbrella. Strings hang below the bell. These are called **tentacles**.

A jellyfish's tentacles hang down from the bell.

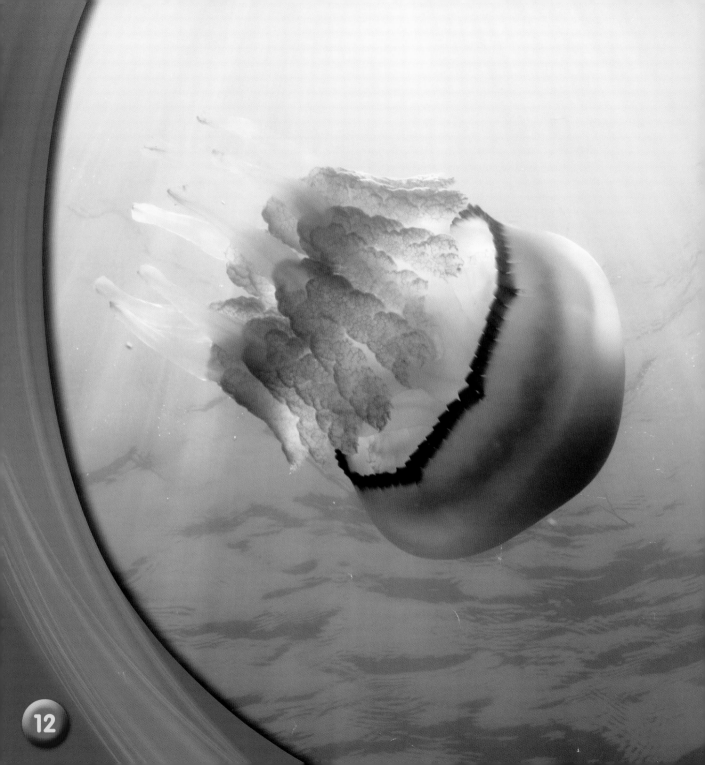

When a jellyfish wants to swim, it uses the bell. The bell squeezes in. Then it relaxes and spreads out. Squeeze and relax. Squeeze and relax.

MAKE A GUESS!

Can you think of any other sea animals with tentacles? Why do they need tentacles? What do they use them for?

A jellyfish uses its bell to swim.

Jellyfish are slow swimmers. Mostly, they move up and down in the water. They do not swim sideways very well. Instead, they let the waves push them around.

Jellyfish usually move wherever the water takes them.

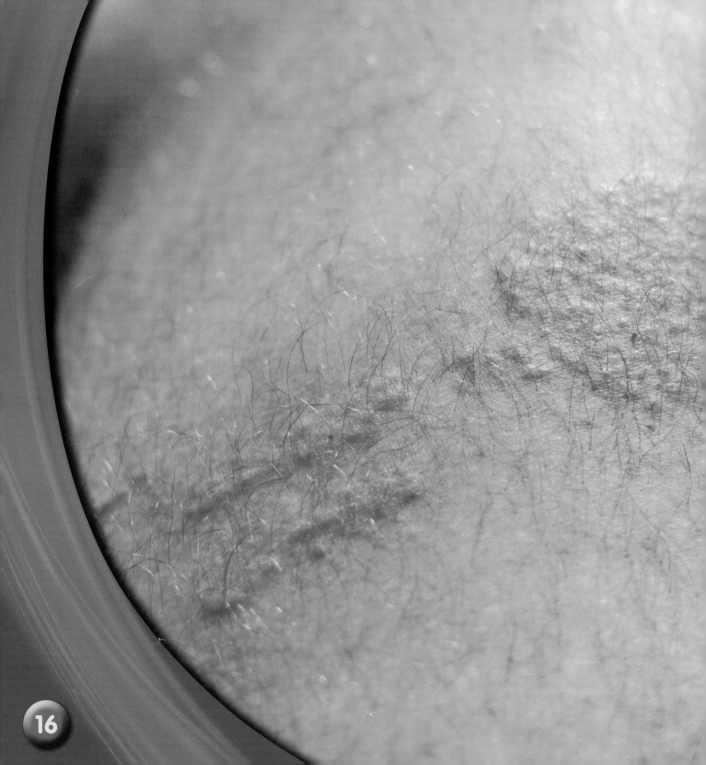

Tentacles do not help the jellyfish swim. Tentacles are loaded with stingers. They sting animals that come too close. This protects the jellyfish from harm. They also use their tentacles to capture **prey**.

This person has been stung by a jellyfish.

So Many Jellyfish

There are many different kinds of jellyfish. They come in all sizes. The biggest ones are the size of washing machines. The smallest ones could fit on a spoon.

This jellyfish has short tentacles compared to its bell.

Some jellyfish are colorful. Their bells have spots or stripes. But most jellies are white or **colorless**. Big, small, colorful, or clear—all jellyfish are interesting animals.

ASK QUESTIONS!

Would you like to learn more about jellyfish? Ask an older family member to help you find more online.

This jellyfish has a pattern of stripes and dots.

21

Think About It

The body of a jellyfish is made up mostly of water. Do you think jellyfish taste good to other animals? Why or why not?

Would a jellyfish make a good pet? Why or why not? Believe it or not, some people do keep them! Go online with an adult to find out how to take care of them.

Sometimes people cook jellyfish to eat. Would you try a bite of one? Why or why not?

Find Out More

BOOK
Spilsbury, Louise. *Jellyfish*. Chicago: Heinemann Library, 2011.

WEB SITE
National Geographic Kids: Giant Jellyfish Invasion
http://kids.nationalgeographic.com/kids/stories/animalsnature/ giant-jellyfish-invasion
Read about a giant jellyfish swarm.

Glossary

bell (BEL) the round, umbrella-shaped part of a jellyfish

colorless (KUHL-er-lehss) clear, or having no color

drift (DRIFT) to float in any direction

prey (PRAY) animals that are eaten by other animals

swarms (SWARMZ) large groups of many animals

tentacles (TEN-tuh-kuhlz) stringy, stinger-filled parts of jellyfish

Index

About the Author

Susan H. Gray is a zoologist. She has written many books about animals. She lives with her husband, Michael, in Cabot, Arkansas. They have many pets but have never owned a jellyfish.